The TREE of Life and WISDOM

The TREE of Life and WISDOM

J. W. BURGESS

BCL
PUBLISHING
KNOXVILLE, TENNESSEE

BCL
PUBLISHING
KNOXVILLE, TENNESSEE

BCL Publishing, LLC
632 Cheowa Circle
Knoxville, TN 37919

Printed in the United States of America.
First edition: 2021
10 9 8 7 6 5 4 3 2 1

ISBN: 978-0-578-31483-9 (Hardcover)
ISBN: 978-0-578-31484-6 (E-book)

Publisher's Cataloging-in-Publication data

Names: Burgess, J. W., author.
Title: The tree of life and wisdom / J. W. Burgess.
Description: Knoxville, TN: BCL Publishing, LLC, 2021.
Identifiers: ISBN: 978-0-578-31483-9 (hardcover) | 978-0-578-31484-6 (ebook)
Subjects: LCSH Burgess, J. W.--Spiritual life. | Spiritual biography. | BISAC BIOGRAPHY & AUTOBIOGRAPHY / Religious | RELIGION / Essays | RELIGION / Spirituality
Classification: LCC BR1725 .B78 2021 | DDC 277.3/0825092--dc23

Cover and interior design by Dexterity, in partnership with Sarah Siegand.

TABLE OF CONTENTS

For our four daughters

Jessica, Jennifer, Alex, and Lindsey

INTRODUCTION

THE TREE OF LIFE AND WISDOM

Around age ten, my boyhood friend and I would take a red wagon and pick up the red and dark-purple berries from underneath his mulberry tree. This was a special tree, the only one we knew of that gave us sweet berries. As I look back on it now, it reminds me of the Tree of Life. Some of our early hunter-gatherer ancestors knew the importance of trees. They would gather their many varieties of fruit and find shelter under the branches of the great trees. The forest, the trees have been life to many of our ancestors from all over the earth.

Humans have felt the living connection to trees for a long time and have made special symbols of trees for religion, health, life, and wisdom. Tree-worshiping cults have been traced back to 10,000 BCE. From the cultures of Ancient Mesopotamia dating 2000 BCE, various trees have served as icons of immortality. Job in the Hebrew Bible opines on the immortality of trees when he contrasts their regenerative life with the brevity of human life.

Under the Bodhi tree, Buddha found enlightenment. The author of Proverbs proclaims, "Wisdom is a tree of life to those who embrace her; happy are those who hold her tightly" (Proverbs 3:18). For me, the wisdom of oneness with all things started with trees.

The most familiar Tree of Life to Western civilization is the one in the Garden of Eden, the paradise of God. There were two trees in the garden; the other was the Tree of Knowledge (wisdom). I have combined both in the title of this book, *The Tree of Life and Wisdom*. Humans ate of the knowledge tree and gained consciousness, self-awareness, and the capacity for wisdom. But the Elohim cast them out so they would not gain immortality. As the Bible closes its metanarrative in the final book of the Christian canon, Revelation, the visionary author sees the righteous nations eating from the fruit of the Tree of Life in the new Jerusalem, the eternal-earthly kingdom of God.

As a preacher boy, I sermonized many times to the garden and the large oak trees in my parents' backyard. In middle life, trees grew in importance to me as I felt the connection to their energy in meditation. I continued my practice of talking to them and began to hug them. Even today I walk out into my backyard of hundred-year-old poplars and place my hand on them to connect to their energy.

My love of trees is not only outdoors; every room of our house is also furnished with solid-wood furniture, as well as a collection of wooden boxes with symbols of the Tree of Life scattered about. So of course, when thinking about the title for this collection of essays dedicated to my daughters, it was obvious that it would be *The Tree of Life and Wisdom.*

It also seemed appropriate to open this collection of essays with a painting by one of my favorite local artists, Jonathan Howe. Jonathan told me the story about his version of the Tree of Life. His painting was the result of a dream, a vision. In his dream, a place of grayness and dead trees was transformed into bright colors when he began worshipping Jesus, and the trees came alive with music. Note how the hands coming out of Jonathan's Tree of Life have the motion of playing the violin. The Divine Harmony has resurrected a dying world.

As I contemplate my life, I, too, feel resurrected from the grayness of religion into the colorful, artful, walking with God. A harmony of divine presence gives me life and wisdom on the journey.

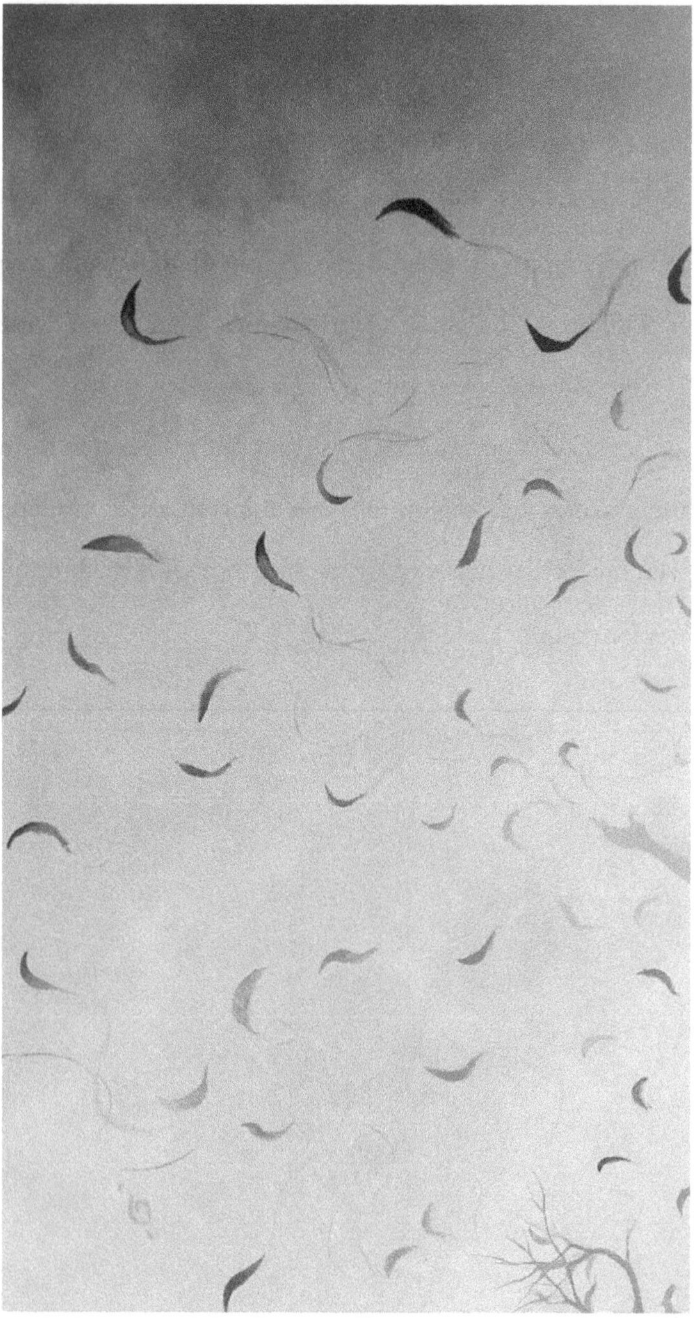

EVENING STAR

Do not cry for me,

But cry,

Cry for the loss you feel.

For there is an empty chair,

The me is no more.

Cry for the loss you feel.

The Body has lost its motion,

The Soul with it.

Cry for the loss you feel.

Now… look to earth and sky,

Stardust has returned to earth,

Spirit and Soul to the evening Star.

My First Theological Lesson

My brother and I, ages six and nine, were two of the few parishioners still in our seats. The rest of the congregation of about forty adults and children had gone to the altar below the pulpit. The atmosphere was noisy and nearly chaotic. The folks at the altar were kneeling or lying on the floor, slain by the Holy Ghost. My family was attending a Sunday evening service at the Church of God in Wilmington, Illinois.

My younger brother was looking at me for some direction. Looking in his eyes, I could interpret the question on his mind. Should we go to the altar and join Mom, Dad, and sister? I sat there feeling the pressure of being the older brother. In addition, I was feeling the group peer pressure to accept the Holy Ghost. My desire to help my brother was primary. The conundrum about the Spirit was simple. I did not feel the Spirit Ghost and I had some doubts about the benefit of shouting "praise God" and wailing at the altar. The cries of the congregation sounded more like fear than relief.

Churchgoing was a staple in our household—that is, for my mom and her three children. My dad, not a churchgoer but a bar-hopper, occasionally joined the family church ritual, usually prompted by guilt. My mom came from a long line of spiritual Alabama women—women who took their relationship with God very seriously. In fact, spiritual worship was necessary sustenance to their soul and emotional stability. The roots of Mom's faith went back several generations to the Holiness Church of Christ, an emotionally demonstrative fundamentalist congregation not so different from our Wilmington Church of God. We were Alabama transplants to the northern region of the country. My dad moved us to Illinois in 1955 when I was two years old to find a good paying industry job.

As the atmosphere in the service became more electrified by the Holy Ghost, I decided my brother and I should retreat to the boys' bathroom. In the bathroom, my brother was still looking for an answer from me. "Are we gonna go up front or not?" he asked.

I vividly recall my answer: "Nope. This seems fake to me." We remained in the bathroom awhile and then returned to our seats. Eventually the emotion in the service subsided.

I have often thought about what prompted me to resist such group peer pressure at the age of nine. At some point before this particular Sunday night, I had formed a sense of freedom, a sense of independence that set me apart from what others thought. This was probably a result of feeling the need for self-sufficiency within my family. My parents behaved like young teenagers. My mom, a simple and sweet young woman; my dad, an angry young man. I felt like I was raising them instead of the other way around. As I observed their immaturity, I had intuitively concluded I should think for myself and not trust emotions to lead to right thinking.

After the service, there was no family discussion about why I did not join in the spiritual festival. I think it was assumed by my parents that if the Holy Ghost did not move me, then I should not go forward. They respected my decision as much as they would any adult. As the oldest, I was raised to be responsible for myself and my two siblings. Like much of my childhood, I would make my own decisions and be responsible for myself. I would also remain skeptical of emotional displays in and out of church.

But what about my parents? Was this emotional ecstasy helpful to them? Unfortunately, my dad's relief from guilt was temporary; it was not long before he returned to his life of self-centered abusive behavior. Perhaps this hypocrisy was another reason such emotional outbursts in church felt fake to me. My mom, on the other hand, found her daily hope in her emotionally based, simple faith. The life of a submissive southern woman was not easy. Of course, three small children before the age of twenty-one added to the complexity of her situation and limited her options. But Mom always found relief in her emotional and spiritual connection to others. Even today, with Jesus in her heart, she cheerfully walks the halls of her nursing home, talking to each neighbor.

It turned out that my rationalist mind would be my guide throughout the next four decades of life. This rationalism would lead me to better choices than my parents. For example, I would eventually do well in school and go to college.

However, my stoic lack of emotion would not serve me so well. I would become dogmatic and enter adulthood thinking I could figure everything out in my own mind. I would pretend empathy for others but rarely feel it. I made my own success; surely other people could do the same. For a long time, I did not realize that self-sufficiency could be taken too far. For a long time, I would remain emotionally cut off from others, living in the solitude of my mental cave. It would be middle life before I walked out of the cave, embracing the value of an open mind and a warm heart.

THE CAVE

The end of my marriage blew a giant hole through my soul. It had lasted thirty-seven years, and we had raised two lovely daughters. In the last step, in mediation, we found ourselves with lawyers going back and forth, negotiating between my feelings of sadness and her feelings of rage.

The caves we crawl into lay deep within the recesses of our mind. My most familiar cave was one of emotional withdrawal. I learned in childhood that the cave provided safe harbor. As a young teenager, the cave provided a sense of self-reliance. In young adulthood, when I married, I discovered self-reliance could be a curse and the emotionless cave a stormy sea.

My sin was a pattern of living emotionally alone. Early in the marriage, my preoccupation with academic degrees and climbing the corporate ladder cheated us of time together. I let my daily schedule of working, studying, and struggling push out the time where friendship should have rooted. Our weekdays were long and our words were few. Weekends were some better, but not enough better to have filled in the gaps of missed intimacy—husband and wife in name only. And two shall remain two.

Eventually children came along and so did all the demands of parenthood. This focus on children reduced our marriage to mere transactions. This joyless living went on month after month, year after year until the years became decades. For us, the idea of "Love Story" was a movie myth.

The years of my preoccupation with education and career wore on the marriage. Drip by drip bitterness and sadness, like stalagmites in a cave, built up inside us. When we talked about our marriage, the conversations were like speaking to each other in a foreign language. She would complain of a "lack of real conversation." I would reply, "I thought we could work things out."

Eventually, her bitterness exposed itself in angry outbursts. Finally, her anger and my sadness took a toll on our respect for whom we had become. However, we did not seek an end to the unhappiness for years; our children and an evangelical background held us to the marriage contract.

Step-by-step hope faded. No matter how good the intentions were, the numbness won. The die was cast. The attorneys were called. The canvas of my life was painted black and white.

The change I needed would not come until my middle years. I began to see myself for what I was: a rationalist estranged from my emotions. I did not like who I had become. I struggled deep within myself, and in the depths, I found repentance. At the time I was attending an evangelical megachurch. The minister was especially bright and articulate. His Sunday evening sermons began to bring up the relational connection to the Holy Other, versus the embracing of religion with its propositional doctrines. I began to listen, to really listen, only to discover that my youthful warm feelings about God had been lying fallow, like the empty fields in my childhood home of Alabama biding time until the next cotton planting. The dam that contained my sea of emotion broke and flooded my life. For two years, it was difficult to attend a service without publicly weeping.

In the solitude of my sorrow and the stillness of meditation, grieving for the damage caused by my emotionless cave and compassionless heart, I discovered I was not alone. I did not have to navigate life by myself. My childhood self-reliance was an illusion. From deep within my being, at the very center of myself—that is, my Self—I perceived something greater. My Self gave witness to my thoughts, and I felt unspeakable peace and connection, at one with consciousness and the energy of nature. The spirit was in everything. My soul filled with joy as I became aware of Self and connection with the spirit that did not require me to sign on to doctrines or propositional statements.

One day, after leaving my emotional cave and my evangelical church, a new conversation started. The words flowed from my pain as another soul listened with her heart. We exchanged words, feelings, stories. Soon the lifeless days were turned into the freshness of new lyrics. I felt the emergence of a lively duo. The thrill of knowing someone whose fountain, as the old Sunday school song goes, flows deep and wide.

I learned in this new relationship to be open and free, to tell all, to hear all. I would experience magic in a thousand conversations. The relationship would grow from the stuff that best friends were made of: joys and sorrows shared, word to word, flesh to flesh, the soul-like dance of two as one. A black and white canvas now covered with color—bright tones of red, yellow, green, and blue. And the two became one.

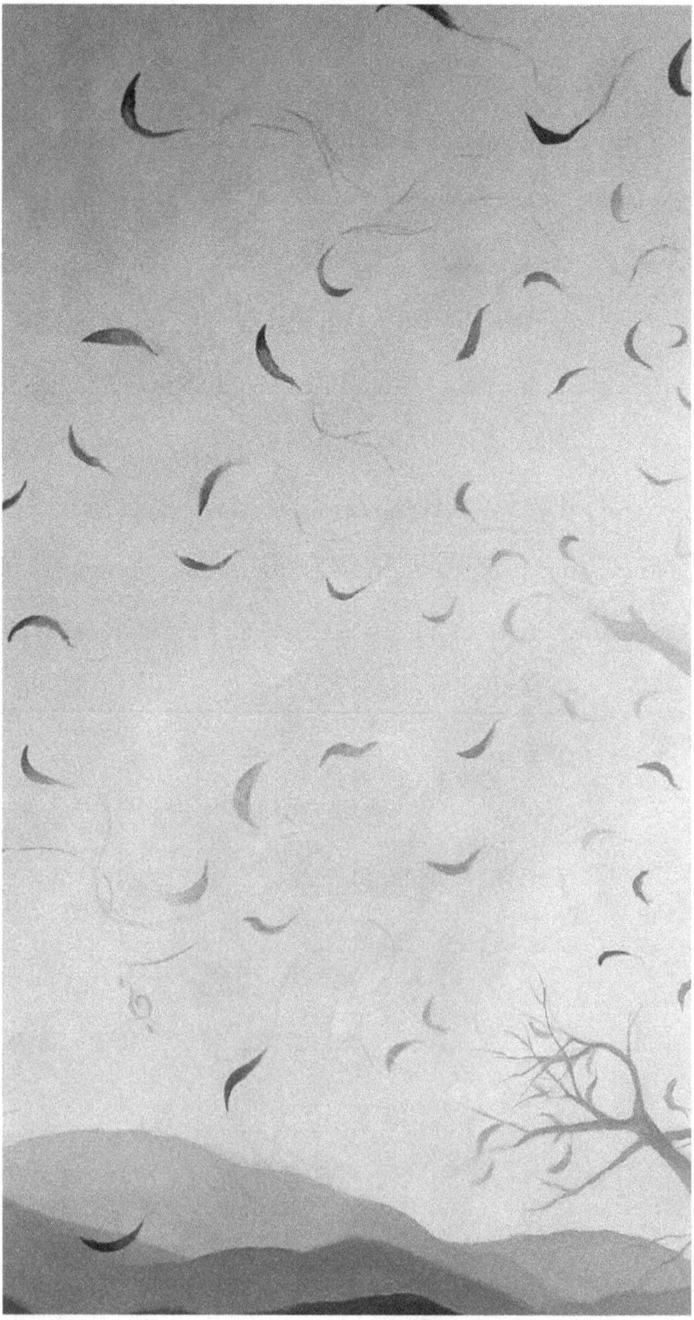

OM AND THE SOUND OF SILENCE

Walking through the windowless spaces and row after row of blinking machines creates an exciting environment for a gambler. There is a machine to fit every budget: a penny, a nickel, a quarter, and for the high roller, dollar machines. With the drop of a coin, the player stares at the whirling images, looking for a winning combination. A thousand machines blinking, clicking, dinging, and ringing, each with its own rhythm, create a jazz symphony of ultimate entertainment.

In its heyday, the casino in Tunica, Mississippi, just south of Memphis, was a busy place. Thousands of middle-class midwestern and southern folks, many retired, gathered for their weekly, monthly or—like me—quarterly gambling fix; there is the rush of the adrenaline throughout the body and when you win, ecstasy!

Two years before this casino trip, I was in the shower at home, my thoughts preoccupied with developing a practice to clear my mind of words. This was a real challenge for someone who lived in his mind and rarely in the present moment, a sort of pondering professor type. I had come to trust my inner thoughts—the rumination, the cogitating—until the problems of life and work were resolved. But now, I was trying to stop thinking about thinking.

I had tried this many times before in the privacy of my daily shower, for the most part unsuccessfully. I had read in my growing library of Eastern meditation that when you do not succeed at blanking your thoughts, just simply try again. I am, if nothing else, stubborn—or perhaps persevering. I am not sure where the line is between those words.

One morning while trying to stop the mindless chatter, a thought emerged: "Why don't you try sound?" If I uttered a sound and repeated it over and over maybe, just maybe, it would drown out the chatter. Besides, I think I had read somewhere that meditators use the sound "om." My ruminating mind said, "Wait a minute. You have kept your meditation practice private, knowing if your family heard you, they would think you've lost your religion and your mind."

Oh, well. Like most times in this situation, I tried it anyway. Om, breath, om, breath, om, breath. Over and over I made the sound between deep breaths. Months of morning showers would pass where I would make the funny sound and try, try to eliminate the chatter. Eventually, slowly, some progress was made—at first for only a few moments, yet long enough that I could sense that the chatter, the thinking, the words were gone. Soon these few seconds of emptiness turned into a half minute, then a minute, then several minutes.

The absence of words put me in the moment. The empty space filled me with peace. I had been a Christian for a long time but never understood, until now, Paul's phrase, "the peace of God, which surpasses all understanding"

(Philippians 4:7, New King James Version). In the shower in a trancelike-state with the water pouring down my back, I understood not with words but with silent knowing.

All my life I had intellectually searched for God within my books, in the propositions of scholars and the dogma of church. Now, in the thoughtless space of inner awareness, the sense of oneness with ultimate consciousness was real. It was not real because it was proven, but real because experientially I came to know consciousness. One medieval text called it "the cloud of unknowing." I was in a place beyond words, thoughts, church, creeds, and my ego.

Om, breath, om, breath, om breath. Chatter gone. Present now. Energy felt, awake to Self.

I usually got a room at the casino and stayed a couple of nights. My game was Texas Hold'em. The poker room with its library look of wooden tables was in stark contrast to the bright, noisy atmosphere of the main floor of slot machines. In this quiet place, dozens of skilled poker players would sit for hours. It was not unusual for one or two tables to play all night. Each table typically had ten players.

The number 1 seat was to the left of the dealer, who sat on one side of the large, green felt table.

I sat there at the $100 buy-in table, a small stakes table, playing, thinking, and gazing at other players. There was not much talk but lots of ego in the atmosphere. I sat and played for twelve hours after having arrived around noon. Poker can be boring if you go a couple of hours without an adrenaline fix. When this occurs, you begin to realize that you are tired. By midnight I was in that exhausted state. "Well, time for me to turn in. See you guys in the morning," I said as I parted. I walked through the noisy main floor of jazz-playing machines, which seemed a half mile of circular walking. Finally, I found the correct bank of elevators, stepped on, and pushed eleven. I went to my room and slept well.

The next morning I woke early, eager to take my shower, skip shaving, dress, find a good breakfast, and return to the tables for my fix and, I hoped, the ecstasy of winning. In the shower, after two years of self-training, meditation was a ritual. I would meditate, find the peaceful silence, witness myself not thinking, calm and sacred energy flowing from my raised hands. Om, breath, om, breath, om, breath. Chatter gone. Present now. Energy felt, awake to Self. Oneness.

Then it happened. There in a casino hotel room. There with water pouring down my back. The energy felt as if an inside power had taken control of my body. The shaking started in my hands but quickly spread to my legs and then my entire body, getting more intense and uncontrollable. This shaking had only happened one other time. On that occasion, I was scared and asked for it to stop and it did. But then I thought later I should not have asked it to stop, because the warm afterglow was pure joy. So, this time, I did not ask for it to stop.

How long the shaking continued, I do not know, but it was less than ten minutes. As the shaking subsided, I felt the warm compassionate glow increasing inside of me—a feeling that would last for two or three hours. When the shaking faded, my mind was filled with wisdom-thoughts. I jumped out of the shower, naked and wet, ran to the table for a pen and paper, and scribbled down the wisdom-thoughts before they disappeared into my subconscious memory. One of those thoughts was, "The great spirit of ultimate reality is subtle and submerged under our daily life."

The joy, warmth, compassion, and sacred peace continued just as intense but without the shaking. I was in a fully alert state of mind. I dressed, skipped shaving, picked up my room key, and opened the door. The entrance was partially blocked by the cleaning cart and there stood the cleaning lady. I looked at her, and for no explainable reason, my heart was overwhelmed with compassion. I pushed back the tears and said with a big smile, "Hello, how are you?"

With a big smile, she replied, "Fine, thank you."

I moved on, afraid to say more. I might start crying, and then who knows what this wonderful cleaning lady might think. I continued down the hall, got on the elevator, and pushed the button for the main floor. As I stepped off the elevator, a man stepped on. I smiled, said, "Hi," and felt the same overwhelming, unexplainable compassion for him. I thought to myself, This is weird, walking around the casino with glowing compassionate feelings for total strangers. It was weird and joyful and peaceful and full of warm energy.

As I approached the poker room counter in an aura of glow, I asked for my usual $100 table, but none were available. I was told there was one seat available at the big stakes table. I needed $500 to have a reasonable stake at this table. So, I decided I would take this seat, but I said to the poker room manager, "Please put me down for the $100 table, and as soon as a seat becomes available, I would like to move."

I took my seat at the big table and ordered $600 worth of chips. The chips came quickly via the chip runner. I tipped him, and I was all set for my gambling fix. At the table were nine players, many of whom had been there all night. This table had not broken up since the evening before. Sitting in seat number 3 was the obvious all-night winner, and in front of him was $10,000 worth of chips. I could tell he was in the rush of adrenaline. As most winners are, he was talkative. In seat number 5 sat a small-built quiet man about my age, in his late forties. He looked fresh; he had not been at the table long. I felt drawn to him, although the compassion was not quite as strong as it had been with the cleaning lady and the stranger at the elevator.

I was seated in my least favorite seat, number 10, next to the right armpit of the dealer. Usually, I have a little anxiety when I first sit down to play poker, especially at a high stakes table, but not this time. I was feeling the same peace I had felt since the shaking experience. The warm glow was still there; I felt confident.

A hand was dealt. Each player received two hold cards that only they saw. The dealer then put three community cards faceup on the green felt. The betting started. When my turn came, I folded my two bad cards. The hand ended quickly, with little consequence. The next round was dealt and ended with a similar outcome. The third hand was dealt. I was holding two small cards, not suited and not connectors (in numerical sequence), again bad cards. This time the chip leader who had been winning all night made a big bet after the first three community cards were laid on the table. The chip leader's bet indicated he probably held something good, maybe a high pair. The quiet man, in seat 5, called the big bet. Ah, this meant he must have a good hand, perhaps better than a pair. Everyone else before me folded. Now in the last seat, it was my turn to act. This should, once again, be another easy fold for me. The only thing I could make that might be the winning hand would be a straight. To make a straight, I needed one of the fours in the deck to show up on the next community card, called the "turn card."

The warm glowing energy was still strong in my soul when, at this moment, I had a brief vision: I saw the four of spades in my mind's eye. Wow! This meant, if I trusted the vision, that my straight was coming and I would have the best hand possible, given the other cards on the board. In poker lingo, I would have "the nuts." The vision was strong, and I felt peace about making an irrational poker move: to "call" the bet, foolishly risking over a hundred dollars to see the next card. I put my chips in and called the bet. The dealer laid the fourth card on the table. Sure enough, it was the four of spades. I had made my straight.

Before the final and fifth community card was dealt, the chip leader was up to bet again. Hoping he still had the best hand and determined to push us out, he went "all in."

This means all his chips were in the pot and to call meant you had to push all your chips into the pot, too. Of course, what he did not know was that the quiet man had him beaten, and that I had the quiet man beaten.

All three of us had all our chips in the pot. When the fifth card was dealt, it was what is known in poker as a blank, meaning it did not change the status of the hand. All three of us showed our cards, and indeed I had "the nuts." The dealer pushed the mountain of chips, worth over $2,000, toward me. I was simultaneously filled with poker ecstasy and sacred energy. At that very moment, the desk called my name over the speaker. There was a seat for me at the small stakes table. I peacefully, mindfully, picked up my winnings and headed to a cheaper table.

Om, breath, om, breath, om, breath. Chatter gone. Present now. Energy felt, awake to Self. Silence.

MONASTERY OF HERETICS

It is not easy to admit the truth to yourself. You know it but you do not say it. Then one day you do say it out loud, but quietly, to yourself. The truth is out of the bag for your Self to see.

You find a friend; you whisper the truth to him. He whispers back, and now you are really scared. What if it is true that the Bible is not always true? What do I do then? I cannot tell them. They will shun me. They will wipe the dirt off their evangelical sandals and be done with me.

I was one of the twelve elders in my megachurch—an insider, so to speak. They prayed hard, they raised their hands, and they cared. Oh, yes, they cared as long as you believed. I went to their meeting, knowing the end for me was near. I was now sucked into the truth that was supposed to make me free. I had to say it. Out loud in a meeting of elders. I knew in the end they would do God's dirty business and try to make me the heretic.

***

My tires made that grinding sound on the gravel road to the inn keeper's office at Shaker Village. It was several months after the excommunication. I was still feeling the heretic's shame.

Shaker Village was an earthy place, full of color and life—thousands of acres of rolling pastures in the heart of Kentucky. The buildings on the site had laid in decay for seventy-five years until a nonprofit foundation in the 1960s rebuilt thirty-four of the original structures, preserving the village as a living museum to this peculiar group of people. The buildings were massive three-story structures of stone and brick. The Shakers (the United Society of Believers in Christ's Second Appearing) were planning for the long haul, a thousand years of Utopia before the second return of Christ. This settlement was built along a gravel road that had been a highway back in the 1800s and a crossroads during the Civil War. The Shakers, pacifists, helped both sides with food and medicine even though they favored the anti-slavery Union and were friends of President Lincoln.

The generations of Shakers that lived here were inventive and prosperous farmers. Life was made up of hard work, worship, and sometimes boredom. The Shakers, who practiced celibacy, recruited orphans, single moms, and widowers to replenish their numbers. But eventually the labor was too hard for the few remaining, and the village succumbed to the Industrial Revolution that made their agrarian way of life economically unsustainable.

My room was in one of the former family dwelling houses that could accommodate a hundred same-gender Shakers back in its day. It was a plain room with simple furnishings fit for its earthy surroundings. The Shakers were well known for their solid wood, straight lines, handcrafted, practical furniture. The antique reproduction furniture was sparsely placed on the hardwood floors in the room with Shaker-green trim and high ceilings. A monastery for heretics.

I carried my few belongings and a box of books into the room and was prepared to stay quiet and silent for a week. My faith had been deconstructed like the once-decaying Shaker buildings. I had retreated here to this peaceful, soulish place to come to terms with the sadness and fear brought on by the dirty business of God's people. My life had been pruned from the megachurch and separated from God's kingdom.

Each morning I rose to fresh country air and a warm spring sun. I dressed and went to the five-star country breakfast offered in the Shaker restaurant. The restaurant was a brief walk down the gravel road to what was originally the Village Elder House. The Shakers were governed by four of their own, two males and two females—ahead of their times on gender equality. These four lived separately in their own massive house. The Elder House now provided a pleasant atmosphere for the serving of three hearty meals a day to the guests. Breakfast was my favorite: bacon, eggs, pastries, fruit, and homemade biscuits with preserves, all served like gourmet country food.

After breakfast I would set up a table and chair under

one of the great oak trees outside the huge house where I was staying. It was on the gravel road, which was the main walking path from building to building. A few tourists taking in the history and culture of the Shakers walked up and down the road. Very few spoke to me, and I returned the silence. The tours were informative and quietly interesting. One could visit the broom-maker's shop, the soap-maker's shop, the wood-maker's shop, the laundry shop, or the herbal shop. My favorite was the meeting house where the Shakers held their spiritual service. The men and women would sit on opposite sides of this great room and sing Shaker songs with lovely voices—a soothing music until the spirit started to energize the worshippers. The energized Shakers would dance solo, and some would break into shaking, hence the nickname given to them by their English critics.

For me, every morning and afternoon contained rounds of reading, thinking, writing, and crying. I cried for the friends I had lost. I cried for the family that shamed me. I cried for my untethered soul. I cried for the pain that deconstruction brings to one's roots. I cried that decades of being a teacher and minister among the evangelicals had come to a sudden, jolting stop. I had tried to cease my questioning of the doctrines of the megachurch, but the elders were right: it was a *slippery slope.* Once I began the journey of open-minded questioning, the road branched simultaneously in a dozen directions. My addiction to truth was in control of my mind and feelings. Each day I would finish a page or two, edit, re-edit, and so on until I was satisfied that I had been as honest as I could be about my questions and my feelings. I did this for five days.

On the final day, I decided to visit the Shaker graveyard about a mile down the gravel road. My emotions were somber but more settled than the other days: less crying, more healing. An old iron fence surrounded the plot of land, with large oaks on its green lawn and a hundred gravestones awkwardly shifted by decades of seasonal rains. Time and weather had faded most of the gravestones. I could barely make out some of the named souls that lay under the cold, grassy ground.

As I stood in the graveyard musing about each Shaker represented by their headstone—babies, women, men, one former slave—I wondered, Where were the Shakers now? Their molecules decayed, given back to the earth. Had the deconstruction of their bodies given new life? Was some of the decay now part of the life in the towering oak trees? Was nature's cycle of life-death-decay-new-life on display? The village had gone through a similar fate over the last two hundred years—its own recycling of buildings and people. Human lives also have a rhythm, a cycle of order, disorder, reorder.

The gentle breeze pushed my graying hair as I stood on the hilltop overseeing the collection of buried bones. I had no answers anymore, only questions. I had no friends, only books. I had no faith, only doubts. Here in this graveyard of decay, I thought about the end of the Shakers, my fellow heretics. They were persecuted from England to America, from town to town, before they found their peace, here, at Pleasant Hill, Kentucky, where they built their village and rebuilt their lives. Here they prospered and died; here they would shake in spiritual ecstasy.

I bent down and picked up an acorn and rubbed it on my blue jeans, a seed for new life. Decay and destruction had come to the Shakers. From the bricks and stones and parts that remained, a group of visionary people had rebuilt the village to share with the world the journey of these communal heretics.

With the parts of me that remained, it was time, time to leave my retreat among the heretical Shakers. Time to move on past God's dirty business. I had come to understand that ultimate answers may always be elusive, but questions were my friends. The journey answered for itself.

THE LETTER M

Joys and sorrows shared, word to word,

flesh to flesh, the soul-like dance of two as one.

As I was waking up in the recovery area, M was bent over near my ear, saying we had bad news. It was a large tumor in my colon. Melanie (I have always called her M) had been trying to wake me for about twenty minutes.

Doctor Tom had visited with M in the waiting room after the colonoscopy and explained the location and size of the tumor. The biopsy results would be back in two days, but he was sure it was cancer. In the meantime, surgery must be immediately scheduled. The tumor was so large it had almost totally blocked the colon. M wept.

The shock of it all continued throughout the day and into the next. It was supposed to be a routine checkup, so how did it turn into this? There really was not much to say. The doctor knew what he saw on the monitor, and the facts were indisputable. I was in a state of shock; it felt surreal, like a dream. It was hard to absorb all the emotion. As a good Zen should, I practiced letting the negative energy pass through me. Just sit and be and take deep breaths, relax, and the energy passes. In the months ahead, I would learn to turn my body over to the medical profession. In the words of Terry Eagleton, in *Reason, Faith, and Revolution*, my soul and body must collaborate as one.

The test results came back, and as suspected, it was cancer, the scary C word. When I heard that word, I was hit with the feeling of mortality. I was later given a quote by a friend who was also a cancer patient: "We are all mortal. Cancer patients just know it is true." I calculated the odds of cancer returning post-surgery and then the odds if I also put my body through chemo (the other scary C word).

I held up four fingers, the odds out of ten that the cancer returns after surgery. If I have chemo, I take one finger down—only three in ten chances the cancer comes back. It was worth the chemo punishment to reduce the odds of developing stage 4 cancer by twenty-five percent. A reasonable but uneasy decision for my soul.

No one can really prepare for the pain right after major surgery. Every nerve hurts like hell. The colon surgery was five hours, a bit longer than expected, and the total time from pre-op to post-op lasted eight hours. It was evening when I woke up in my hospital room with M once again by my side. Holding my hand, M said, "Everything went well, and you are in your room now." There was an IV in my left hand and something else attached to my right arm, someone taking the catheter out, and someone putting some kind of medical device around my legs. I couldn't move my body; it was entangled with tubes, wires, and equipment.

I slipped back into a light, uneasy slumber. But you sleep in segments in a hospital; about every forty-five minutes to an hour, someone enters the room to poke or prod the body—a a continuous flow of nurses and techs. They gave me pills, checked my vitals, drew my blood, and all sorts of other things. Any movement was painful, and any movement was a continuous series of adjustments.

I was immediately expected to get up and go to the bathroom. "The more movement the better," said the nurses. "You will heal faster." Hell, slow healing was OK with me. M and the nurse would assist me to rise from the bed in much pain, walk me to the bathroom in much pain, and stay close outside the door in case I fell. After peeing in much pain, they escorted me back to bed, which required another three dozen painful movements. This went on all night. Techs in. Body moves. Techs out. Body moves. Take a drink. Body moves. Go to the bathroom. Body moves six dozen times there and back.

M and I have always talked a lot with each other. It is the life blood of our soulish relationship. We can talk for hours and not run out of anything to say. We have carried on these long hours of conversations for hundreds if not thousands of evenings. It is quite amazing to me that we always have so much to say. Like a stream of consciousness, one topic rolls into another.

M has a pleasant and present disposition. She is kind, diligent, and an enforcer of medical rules. Her heart aches with deep empathy, yet her mind keeps it all in perspective. A practical and caring soul. I admire that her soul and body seem to be always present in the same place. I knew she would not leave my side until we went home, that we would be in the same place. I also knew that the nights in the hospital would be difficult.

Here we were in a hospital room, me lying in a bed and M, a few feet away, torturously trying to sleep in a chair made into a cot. Both of us were trying to sleep with a constant flow of nurses and techs, with the ebb and flow of conversation and, for me, lots of painful movement. To my surprise, we were able to talk and laugh, although the movement that comes with laughter was, you guessed it, painful. We joked about cancer, mortality, my painful bathroom trips, and more, as if being in the hospital was a lighthearted evening at home in our den. Somehow the bodily pain of the moment was kept at bay with the soulish evening talk.

In the middle of the first night, I got up to go to the bathroom with M's assistance. It was worse this time. I think the pain medicine had just about worn off. On the way back from the bathroom, my body doubled over with pain and tears ran down my cheek as I reached out for M. She grabbed my arm, and tears came rushing out of her soul and into her eyes.

I don't ever remember watching someone else break into tears as they watched me cry. The empathy runs deep in these circumstances. There was a mysterious connection—a bond of energy and life between us. There was no doubt in this revealing moment that M loved me body and soul. And I can only imagine how challenging that can be. She has walked with me through the cool emotional times, the overly rational times, the man-groaning when I have a sore throat times, the thousand and one new idea times, the snoring times, and now through this pain in the hospital.

When I finally made it back to the bed, I maneuvered my body into a crack between my pillow and the right side of the bed. I put my earplugs in to listen to my soulish play list. It helped, and I slipped into a deep sleep. About forty-five minutes later, someone came into the room again. I gradually came out of my sleepy state listening to Mary Chapin Carpenter—a beautifully meaningful song, a song put there by providence:

Fare thee well
My own true love
Farewell for a while
I'm going away
But I'll be back
Though I go 10,000 miles.

The lyrics continue to say that if he doesn't come back, the unimaginable may happen, such as rocks melting and seas burning. And then the poet continues:

Oh, don't you see
That lonesome dove
Sitting on an ivy tree
She's weeping for
Her own true love …

And so it was, 10,000 miles later, my soul and body returned to M. All was not the same, my soul was changed—not by the trauma of the Cs but by the weeping of the M.

SAINTS DRESS IN PINK AND BLACK

The donut reigns at the top of my food pyramid. And as a donut connoisseur, I proclaim that there's no better practitioner of donut-creation than the Blue Ridge Restaurant inside the Grove Park Inn of Asheville, North Carolina. The Grove Park's donut surpasses all other donuts I've encountered during my many travels. The secret is its light cakiness combined with the sweetest of icing. The chocolate icing on top of a chocolate cake donut ranks as the all-time winner. I should also mention that these are not your regular size donuts. Somehow, they are larger but don't make you feel you are eating a large donut, and so you can have two. If you are going to cheat on your diabetic diet, there is no finer food.

Of course, Grove Park means more than donuts to me. For over twenty years I have been visiting Grove Park; it is one of my favorite places. Grove Park holds an especially soft spot in my heart because of the many trips with M during our ten years together. I proposed to her at Grove Park, down below the terrace, sitting by the spa waterfall. Special things happen during visits to Grove Park, including my last visit when I met a saint dressed in a snappy pink and black three-piece suit with a matching pocket handkerchief.

After learning my cancer had returned, M and I decided to cancel our trip to another special place, Mohonk Mountain House in New York. I was now in stage 4 with a much shorter horizon to live. Chemo needed to start soon, so it no longer seemed wise to be gone a week in New York. We opted for a three-day trip to Asheville.

Time slows down at Grove Park, especially if you just hang out and don't try to visit every shop and see every interesting art store in downtown Asheville. We decided to make this trip low key. We'd done most of the other stuff during our previous trips. Now with that said, we could not pass up a visit to the Battery Book Exchange downtown, near the Arcade. The Book Exchange has 37,000 volumes of used and rare books. They also have a wonderful coffee and lunch restaurant inside the shop and out on the bustling sidewalk. M and I are book lovers with 4,000 volumes in our personal library. Wandering around the Battery Book Exchange can go on for hours, which it did, including a delicious lunch.

In the afternoon when we checked into the Grove Park, we requested to stay in our favorite part of the hotel, in a historic room. We have stayed many times on the fourth floor of the main hotel with a grand view of three tiers of the Great Smoky Mountains.

Breakfast at the Blue Ridge Restaurant was included. The restaurant is at the end of the west hall called Sammons, one of two large halls leading from the Great Hall at the center of the lodge. Upon arrival, guests discover a giant rectangular room with a wall of windows overlooking the Great Smokies. The restaurant offers four rooms of food spread out thematically on a dozen tables: hot foods, fruit, cereals, an omelet bar, and a waffle bar. It is the quintessential hearty American breakfast.

In addition to their homemade donuts, they offer another specialty: stone grits, M's favorite. They are the most flavorful she has ever tasted, and I agreed once I discovered that I didn't need to add sugar to them.

Our plan was to rise in the morning and get to breakfast about 8:30 a.m., but this night didn't go as planned. I always get up at least once to go to the bathroom, a male aging thing. And many times, now, I get up for an hour or two in the wee hours of the morning to read and write. This works because I have a desk with a small lamp in a corner of our bedroom at home. And if I am good and quiet, M can roll over and quickly go back to sleep. We had a similar setup in our room at Grove Park.

This Saturday evening was at the close of a wonderful day with M. We had visited the Battery Book Exchange, each of us picking up a few books. We then ate a lovely dinner at the Edison at Grove Park and even enjoyed a romantic evening, which had become redefined given the past year of cancer. We went to bed after talking awhile, our favorite activity together. But I couldn't sleep. I got up, went to the bathroom, and then sat down at the desk on the other side of the room from where M was rolled over away from me.

Unfortunately, some of my positive energy, along with a bit of hope, eroded in my late-night rumination about the shortness of life. Just about a week and a half before this trip to Grove Park Inn, I had been given the latest bad news about my cancer: I was likely to live only a couple of years. After the initial shock and grief, I had determined to double down on my meditation practice and focus positive energy to my liver, the location of the latest tumors.

This had brought me a week of peaceful living just before the trip.

But now, sitting at my Grove Park desk, the focus was on the boxes of time I had drawn in my journal. The first box contained "six months"—the box of no more treatment. The second box, containing "two years," was likely if I stayed under treatment with all of its quality of life issues. And the third box of "five years" was not so encouraging, because only about twenty percent of the folks in my situation make it to five years, and who knows after that. There was little one could feel or think that wasn't negative when coming to the stark box diagrams. It is such a clear picture of a complex set of medical variables—all easy to get lost in—from hard-to-remember names of drug options, to the side effects for each, to the percentages of survival, to the additional medication needed to mitigate the side effects. Maybe worse is that there are months of waiting to hear if any of this is working.

My thirty-five years of business thinking leads me to take a set of variables and clarify the options, even to the point of oversimplification. I take problems and determine logical sets of options, assigning statistical probability. This served me well as a health-care business strategist. Combined with my intuitive and subjective meditation experience over the last seventeen years, I am a right- and left-brain problem solver, a strange combination of both objectivity and subjectivity, both sides of human nature.

Eventually I tired and went back to bed with my

hopeful spirit eroded. I fell asleep for a couple of hours; then a nightmare startled me and I woke again. Nightmares were common for me during the first round of stage 3 chemo treatment. I had never been prone to nightmares, but cancer changed that. And even though I wasn't on my next round of chemo until Monday morning, the nightmares had started back with the inevitable, pending prospects of more to come.

As I woke up this time, I unfortunately stumbled out of bed and hit my head on the side table. My cry of "ouch" woke M, of course. Now we were both awake two hours before the alarm. A bad thing for M, who requires seven to eight hours of sleep, like normal people who want to have a physically restful existence. Embarrassed, I said, "M, go back to sleep; it's only a little blood." Of course, this was a joke, and given she was already awake because of my clumsy act, I wanted to make her laugh. She did not laugh, and she did not believe me, and she did not go back to sleep. Instead, she was awake with a less hopeful husband than she had gone to sleep with. Her sweet compassion kicked in, and she was willing to trade precious sleep for therapeutic talk about the box diagram. She realized that I was bothered by the prospects of leaving her too soon. Too soon, requiring her to parent our adult children alone. It is true that "parenting never stops." Quite a burden to leave behind for a partner. After a good talk, we decided to get dressed and go for an energetic walking tour of the grounds. Maybe this would clear our minds of some of the realities we were facing.

This walk paid off; we discovered a mature oak tree by itself, planted in a circular bed of dirt four feet above the surrounding pavement. I commented that it reminded me of one of my favorite symbols, the "Tree of Life." I think M agreed, or at least she agreed to take my picture standing by the tree. After about thirty minutes we wandered into the Blue Ridge Restaurant for our wonderful breakfast containing our favorite foods.

We were seated by a window, and within our view on the grounds below was the designated "Tree of Life." It already felt like it was going to be a special breakfast. Besides, M had already forgiven my trespass of waking her up too early. As we browsed around the dozen tables of delicious breakfast foods, M said with some concern, "I don't see the donuts."

I replied, "Surely you just overlooked them."

After wandering around for about five minutes, checking out every item on every table twice, it was true: no donuts. Now this may seem like a trivial issue to some, but to someone who had put Grove Park Inn donuts on his bucket list, it was a traumatic moment. Oh, well, I had no choice but to fill two plates with food, including stone grits.

M and I returned to our seats with lots of other fine food and a grateful heart that we could be having breakfast with each other, with the Tree of Life just outside our window. However, we also thought it was worth asking the waitress about the missing main course. She replied, "Oh, yes. I think we're going to reintroduce the donuts soon. We've just opened back up to full capacity after COVID. I've had other customers mention the donuts; I'll mention it to management." We thought this was kind of her.

And that's when, a few minutes later, we met the man in the pink and black suit. He had a shaven head and was short, about my height of five feet, seven inches (rounded up). He wanted to know how our meal was. This seemed like the perfect opportunity to mention the best grits in the south and the missing donuts. M said we drove two hours and paid four hundred dollars a night to stay at Grove Park Inn because we wanted a Grove Park Inn homemade donut. His eyes lit up. Frankly, I was surprised that my sweet, diplomatic-to-a-fault wife put the point so directly. Of course, she was correct. The gentleman in snappy colors said, "Give me a minute" and left our table. We thought to ourselves, Can he whip up homemade donuts on the spot?

Before we were into our second round of grazing, the gentleman returned with a box of warm donuts. Wow, we were impressed. We chatted for a few minutes and gave him our hearty thanks. As he turned away, I added, "By the way, we came here this weekend because it really was on my bucket list. I am a cancer patient."

The kind gentlemen turned and walked back to our table and said, "So am I. I had cancer in my lung; it spread to my brain last year."

It is hard to put into words that special moment. I

was filled with empathy for him as I felt his empathy for me. You know it rarely travels in both directions at the same time, but when it does, the power of double energy is felt by both. I think M felt it, too. I heard him relay his cancer story of chemo, radiation, and surgery, going from stage 4 back to stage 3. I knew the stats for this. I had been counting them most of the night.

Here standing in front of me was a person who had been where I am now. He was back to work. He was upbeat and warm. He was finding meaning in every day. He was dressing every day as if there were a party just around the corner.

I could barely hold back the tears as I relayed my cancer story to him.

As we parted I wanted to give him a hug, but the COVID thing got in the way, so I reached out to bump his fist. He kindly returned it even though it might be against policy.

When our waitress returned, we asked her, "Who were we just talking to?"

She said he was the manager of the Blue Ridge and

all the stores in this wing of the hotel. She added, "I hope you mentioned the donuts to him. If anyone can bring them back to the restaurant, he can."

My attitude did an about-face. No longer did I linger in the statistics of probable death. I just felt the glow and restarted my day with meditating about this experience and this saint I had just met. The survivors of stage 4 cancer may be few, but they have names and personalities and are living each day in gratitude, hope, and joy, paying it forward.

But this was not the end of this amazing experience. We were leaving for chemo in Knoxville the next morning at seven sharp and had made our Monday morning plan: rise at 5:45, dress and pack by 6:15, call the valet, pack our car by 6:25, and be at the Blue Ridge for the last breakfast. All went according to plan except, once again, I got up too early for M's comfort.

As we met all our time goals with a few minutes to spare, we were walking down to the restaurant, and there wasn't a soul in sight but one. Yep, the gentleman in pink and black was now walking our way, not in yesterday's pink and black but in another snappy striped and vested suit. He greeted us and asked us what we were doing today. We explained that we were grabbing an early breakfast and heading to Knoxville for chemo. A concerned looked appeared on his face as he said, "The restaurant doesn't open until 7 a.m."

We explained registration had informed us it opened at 6:30. The gentleman once again said, "Stay here and give me a minute." Sure enough, he returned in five minutes, opened the giant wooden, glass-inlaid doors of the Blue Ridge and invited us in. We were directed to a table by the window, where a waitress was ready to serve us.

We proceeded to go around the thematic tables and collect our breakfast, came back to our seats, and ate like VIPs. Soon the gentleman returned and said, "I have more donuts. Here, take this box with you."

We thanked him for the donuts, but much more than that, I thanked him for giving me a bit of hope in a moment when hope seemed far off. He reached out and I shook the hand—not of a restaurant manager, but of a saint sometimes disguised in pink and black.

PEACE AT A WEDDING

It was a wedding celebration. A Sharon family event. Sharon, the matriarch of the Gerkin family, is a person of intense emotions and strong opinions, whether adopting the role of cheerleader, servant, or saint. Unless you have known someone like Sharon, you probably would never believe it possible for one person to feel so strongly about everything.

I entered this family tribe about ten years ago when I married Sharon's biological daughter. At the time, I didn't realize how this would put me in Sharon's crosshairs. Sharon had two other stepdaughters and a deceased stepson, but the apple of her eye was her daughter M.

M tells me how Sharon was always a personality bigger than life. A mother who loved so much that she wouldn't—couldn't—rest until her daughter was pushed to be the best she could be. M's biological father was much different and had a quieter nurturing spirit.

Within the tribe were seven girl cousins, Sharon's granddaughters, who were very close growing up. They were a tight group that Sharon, Grammie, took under her wing to protect and to form in the image of God. Six of the girls came in pairs (the oldest having left home earlier): Samantha/Sarah, Emily/Alex, and the youngest pair, Olivia/Linz. Two of these girls were M's children and my stepdaughters, Alex and Linz.

These six have many Grammie stories, such as the trip to Chicago, when seven people and luggage all piled into one SUV. To this day, the cousins talk about Grammie marching them across Chicago, miles at a time, and the adventure of roaming a big city together. Then there are the many summer pool parties during cousins camp. Grammie was always there for them, meeting their needs physically, emotionally, or spiritually. Grammie was also their friend and remains, for all of them, a treasured grandparent.

Sharon's father is a legend because Sharon can't resist telling a story about him with every visit. He was a Methodist circuit minister from the 1950s until his death in 1991. According to Sharon, he was a saint any way you want to measure it. Sharon, I think, has spent her whole life trying to be recreated in her father's image. I believe only Jesus could compete with Sharon's father as her most important role model, and even then, Jesus might be runner-up.

To express a different opinion from Sharon can feel like an act of courage. You must be polite, loving, and firm. M struggled for years to express herself with her mom; it took her until she was about thirty to learn. Since then, M has learned to differ with the family matriarch with love and diplomacy—being honest and direct even though her natural self wants to be sweet and compliant.

When Sarah, the third oldest of the seven cousins, was getting married, Grammie was right in the middle of it all. In addition to being a wedding, it was to be a family festival. The clan would gather, celebrate Sarah, and partake in food, music, and dance. These events are not optional. If you are a member of the clan, you are expected to be there. An acceptable excuse might be if you are overseas in the military and the government is so rude as to not grant Grammie's request to give you leave. Otherwise, you will be present.

I did have a legitimate excuse to miss this tribal event: I was undergoing chemotherapy, and the treatment would wear me down to the point of making it difficult to dress and get in the car. But on the day of the wedding, it turned out that I felt enough energy to bathe, dress, and celebrate.

The wedding was, in Sarah's words, "simple and quick, the way we do it around here." The wedding took place on the lawn of a beautiful country home by a creek, with a pavilion for the reception. To be outside in the open air on a wonderful spring day put a step in my chemo-fatigued self. I was enjoying feeling well and seeing the family for the first time in over a year. Usually, Sharon would call the tribe together at least three times a year. However, due to COVID, even Sharon had to alter her plans. In hindsight I am a bit surprised she succumbed to the advice of the government.

Just after dinner, as the music and dancing were picking up, Sharon looked at me and said, "I need to talk to you." Well, this is always a cue to a serious conversation. My mother-in-law and I walked out on the lawn away from the noise under the pavilion. When we were far enough away for a private conversation, Sharon began, "I need to know how you are doing?"

I knew this question had triple meaning: How are you feeling physically after your recent chemo treatment? How are you doing emotionally, with the odds against you living more than two years? And how are you doing spiritually, given you don't believe in the traditional doctrines of the church? It was this later question that drove her intensity to talk with me during the wedding celebration.

The answer to the first question was simple enough. I was feeling fatigue, but all in all, the chemo side effects hadn't been bad. The second question was relatively easy as well. I feel positive energy eighty percent of the time. This is mostly true because of my meditation practice, bringing me inner peace. I knew Sharon would like this answer; she believes in positive thinking to the extreme. In fact, I wondered if she had ever really considered the fact that not all humans are eternal optimists and that cheerleading optimism can have its limits?

The third question was the challenging one. Given that Sharon knew I was not a Bible-believing, Jesus-worshipping Christian anymore, she sincerely wondered about my soul. Since she had learned of my dim prognosis, she had been even more concerned about where I might spend eternity.

I knew that if we got stuck on what I did or didn't believe, this conversation would not end well. Both Sharon and I wanted her to find peace about my soul in the afterlife. So I decided that, as much as possible, I needed to use Sharon's language to describe the state of my soul. I began by using the term *Holy Spirit.* Being a mystic, what I experience as oneness with God could be called fellowship with the Holy Spirit. And I could use this phrase without compromising my integrity. This turned out to be common ground between the two of us. Sharon seemed to accept that I might indeed experience the Holy Spirit. As I felt my way along the path of this conversation, it became apparent there was an opening. So, I followed up with, "You know, Sharon. I have experienced this same Holy Spirit since I was a boy."

She followed up with, "Well, I understand you were raised hard as a boy and religion was harsh to you." The implication being that I therefore turned away from the church. But the reality was, as I stated to her, that I did mostly raise myself; however, I had a "sweet mama who loved Jesus and took me to church." We both found consolation in the church to emotionally support us given the harshness of life with my dad. The Holy Spirit and I have always been close, and I've found the experience of the Spirit to be a consolation in life.

Now keep in mind, my typical way of describing this is "in meditation I find a centered place where I encounter my true self and oneness with the universal consciousness." I am more comfortable with these words, but of course Sharon would not be. And this conversation was for her benefit, helping her understand that my soul is at peace with ultimate Reality.

Her response this time was something like, "But . . . you don't believe. . . ." She didn't finish the statement, but what she meant was, "You don't believe Jesus was God." I pushed on with this comment: "Beliefs. There are lots of variation on beliefs, even in your own church or the church you were raised in. Does it really come down to a person's belief, or does it come down to an experiential knowledge of God?"

I have had this kind of experience of God since I was a boy. I have changed what I believe about God many, many times. But to be present with the Great Spirit is the "knowing" of it all. I said a long time ago that I stopped talking about *faith* because I *know* through my experience the Holy Spirit, the ground of being.

"Sharon," I continued, "if I have known the Holy Spirit all this time, don't you think I will be with Him in the hereafter, whatever that looks like?"

After she hesitated, she smiled and nodded yes. In that moment, I knew I had found some common ground on which we both could have peace.

I concluded, "Sharon, you can be at peace about my soul." She agreed and we hugged.

This felt like a good time to emphasize my impending shortness of life to Sharon, the cheerleading optimist. I said, "Sharon, I have but one promise I need from you."

This woman of high integrity said, "Oh, I can't promise until you tell me what it is."

I already knew her answer to the question. This was more about making sure her optimism could accept the reality that life was probably short for me. I said, "Your daughter will grieve; she will need you."

Of course, Sharon answered, "I will be like her rock."

I acknowledged that my daughters would need M to be a rock for them. Knowing that there would be rock behind rock, this gave me great peace. This serious talk at a wedding celebration gave both Sharon and me peace in our souls.

And I added this silent benediction: Blessings on the matriarch who will be a rock for the people I leave behind!

MAGICAL CHILD

The birth of the Magical Child took place at Baptist Memorial Hospital, one of the two major hospital systems in Memphis. At that time, I was an underpaid schoolteacher, but because of the birth of the Magical Child, I would end up working at the other major hospital system, Methodist Health.

I first met the Magical Child in the delivery room, where her beauty was yet to emerge. From my perspective, Jessica looked like all newborns: an ugly duckling. Only mothers seem to see their beauty, and everyone else plays along, saying, "Oh, isn't she so cute?"

It didn't take long for her true beauty to show, along

with the sound of her constant crying. She cried for eight months. I spent many sleepless nights rocking her to sleep as she laid on my stomach. I can't help but think our lifetime of bonding started during these sleepless nights.

Now there were a few times later in her life when you wouldn't think we had ever bonded—like her running to hide when I came home from work. I had expected the opposite reaction from my two-year-old. Or there was the time she broke my heart when she said on her high school graduation day, "Dad, you love Saturday Buddy (her sister) more than me." Or the time she crushed my heart when I divorced her mother and, on the phone, she said, "Fuck you, Dad. Fuck you, dad. Fuck you!" I fell to my condo floor, doubled over, wailing for two hours.

She is the Magical Child but also the Outlaw Child. Let me explain the latter. Her name Jess comes from my grandfather, Jessie James Burgess. Indeed, he was named after the infamous outlaw. Legend has it that after robbing a Huntsville, Alabama, bank, Jessie James jumped off a now famous cliff, horse and all, into a pool of water to evade the law. Jessie James Burgess was called Jess by his friends, and I wanted to use this name for Jessica. Turns out Jess has been a good name; it fits the Magical Child's outsider ways.

My Jess was always coloring outside the lines, finding creative ways to play and dress with style. The girl was always into the trendy and sometimes ahead of the trend. I watched her beauty grow with her good taste. Jess eventually applied her independent thinking and natural creativity to become an entrepreneur. She started her own business and has become a national leader in the event design industry. Her stubborn streak also paid off because even in hard times—and entrepreneurs always have some hard times—she stuck with it.

Jess was raised, unlike me, with lots of advantages, and she thought for a long time she knew almost everything there was to know to live the "good life." Then one day she found herself in divorce proceedings. The divorce shattered her idea of what makes the good life: a good marriage, a big house, new cars, and a cute child.

Another challenge to Jess's good life was the raising of Sullivan, my grandson. Jessica, as a single, self-employed mom, has shown much grace, wisdom, and patience as she helped Sullivan navigate his first eight years of life. I see a sweet inner person in Sullivan and, at the same time, a child bursting with energy he can hardly control.

Now back to the magic of my firstborn. Even before she was born, we knew that we wanted her mom to stay home with her. We were not in favor of someone else raising our daughter. Yet I was an underpaid schoolteacher and her mom needed to work to help pay the mortgage on our simple first home. I felt a heavy responsibility to provide for them both. Under this burden, late one Saturday night, I decided to walk down the street to our church and let myself in to pray at the altar. In essence, I negotiated with the divine. I said, "I am willing to leave the career I love, teaching high school history, to make more money for my family, if you would only help me."

The next night we were at church, and afterward a deacon came up to me and said, "I'm not sure you're in the market, but I know of an entry level job in health care that would pay well. Are you interested?" I took this as a sign, interviewed, and got the job—even with minimum qualifications. Keeping my side of the bargain, I left the teaching career I loved to enter my first health-care job. The divine also kept their side of the bargain: my new job covered the combined salaries of my teaching job and my spouse's banking job to the exact dollar.

So Jessica's mom stayed home with her. And I, over three decades, rose through the ranks to CEO of a health insurance company. Even though it was not my first love, health care was a good career for me. I don't claim to know how providence works, but something sure worked through the birth of the Magical Child to give me a job providing for the family throughout my lifetime.

The Magical Child opened her mind beyond the religious ways she was raised, concluding that church may be the last place someone finds God. It took me twenty years to get to the same point. When I did discover church was not the answer, I began to meditate, which warmed my heart and opened my mind. A spirituality developed inside me, replacing the dull religious tradition in which I was steeped.

A couple of years ago the Magical Child also discovered the power of meditation, releasing negative energy and taking in positive energy. It seemed to increase her artful living. More magic!

We have shared many wonderful conversations about our common approach to spirituality, bonding even closer than when we were in the rocking chair. Her thoughts are a blessing to me, and I think mine are to her. We share our inner wisdom that comes from that centered place within our spirit. The Magical Child is one of my best friends.

The other day I was feeling a bit down as I sat in the waiting room for my next chemo treatment, hoping to slow down my stage 4 cancer. I decided to text Jess: "Could you send me some positive energy the next time you meditate?" She texted back, "I was about to meditate, and you were on my mind, Dad." I came out of the infusion chair with a renewed spirit.

Only days earlier, the daughter that ten years ago said to me, "Fuck you, Dad," sent me a text saying something she had never said before: "I will always love you." My Magical Child may miss me most because she is most like me. The comforting thought is that she will not be alone when I am gone. She will have M as a rock for life.

If there is a spirit afterlife, and I think there is, I will meet my Magical Child at her transition and accompany her to the life beyond.

You are blessed, Magical Child!

SATURDAY BUDDY

Jennifer was born at Christ Hospital, which sits on the highest of the seven Queen City hills in Cincinnati. On the majestic hospital campus was an old chapel, and the cross on the steeple was lit up at night, shining for the whole city to see. I still remember the tears of joy I shed in the delivery room on the night Jen was born.

When she was a toddler, she would crawl back and forth across my back as I lay on the floor reading textbooks for my MBA. She was a cute blonde with my blue eyes that shone like sparklers when we mentioned her favorite toy, Big Bird. She had the biggest smile, even though her two front teeth were crooked due to the constant sucking of her left thumb. The doctor said she came out of the womb sucking that thumb. But this didn't keep her smile, like the Christ Hospital steeple, from lighting up for everyone around her.

Almost every Saturday of her young life we would get in the car to run errands, stopping off for Cincinnati's Skyline Chili and maybe ice cream at Graeter's. This is how Jen became known as my Saturday Buddy. I had thought I wanted a son for our second child, but I was wrong. There is no boy that would have befriended me the way my Saturday Buddy did.

When she was three, I would carry her on my shoulders as she hung on to my hair as if it were a horse's mane. The only time this was a burden was the time halfway through Mammoth Cave when she decided she didn't want to walk anymore, so I had to carry her on my shoulders the rest of the way. It was a long mile and a half, underground through narrow spaces.

Jen wanted to be a dancer, and we gave her dancing lessons. She tried her hardest, but she wasn't the best dancer. However, she was the most liked by her peers. Later, Jen wanted to be a swimmer. Again, she tried her hardest but she was the slowest swimmer on the team, yet again the most liked by her teammates. Jen always persevered at any task she was challenged with, and even though not the best, she hung in there. More importantly she always knew that people were more important than tasks. We got her teeth fixed, and her smile would electrify a room of people, making every person feel like they counted. Of course, it wasn't just the smile but the warm, authentically caring personality behind the smile.

Sometimes while I was driving the car and Jen was sitting in the passenger seat, I would break out in a song like "Amazing Grace." Jen would join in at the top of her lungs, and we would sing and then look at each other with two big smiles beaming out the light of the world. I knew in that moment that I would dread the day my Saturday Buddy grew up and left me. In fact, I must have thought this a hundred times before she was age twelve.

Only a few of us grow up knowing exactly what we want to do in life and then do it. Jen is one of those people.

She wanted to teach children. In fact, she started teaching her stuffed animals the ABCs as soon as she learned them for herself. Jen is connected to life by being connected to others, even if the others are stuffed.

When my Saturday Buddy did grow up and go to college, I grieved for a year. Like everything else in her life, Jen applied herself in college. She completed every assignment to the best of her ability, despite having had a slow start developing her own reading skills in kindergarten. Like her dad, she was a late bloomer and didn't become a competent reader at first. That all changed for her in later elementary school. If there is one thing Jen and I share other than our blue eyes, round faces, big smiles, and love of books, it is our perseverance to do our best. Jen graduated college with honors. My Saturday Buddy was now a beautiful, intelligent, caring young woman, but my mind would frequently flash back to the Saturdays at Skyline Chili or the duo singing in the car.

Jen became a teacher at the school where she did her student teaching. It was a very good school district and usually only hired teachers with experience.

However, they loved Jen and hired her right out of college. She turned out to be one of their outstanding teachers. When Jen earned her master's degree, I remember her struggle with teaching full time and taking graduate classes. But once again she persevered and graduated with honors. Soon after, the school district promoted her to reading coach for the district.

In time my sweet Saturday Buddy found a partner. The couple had a cute little blond girl with blue eyes and the biggest smile, Saturday Buddy Junior. Unfortunately, I don't live close enough to adopt Addie Mae as my Saturday Buddy. However, and better yet, she has become her mom's Saturday Buddy. When I see them together, I flash back once again to those precious and fleeting days.

I see it: the crawling, the sweet chatter, the fun disposition. It is all there once again, embodied anew in Addie Mae. There is no doubt Addie Mae will bring great joy to her parents and many others throughout her life just like my Saturday Buddy has done and will continue to do. Not all parents are as lucky as me, to have a child who enjoys their company so much that they just hang out in childhood, in adolescence, and occasionally now in adulthood.

Sometimes Jen will sign a card to me, "Your Saturday Buddy." That makes the rest of the days of my month feel like Saturdays, too.

WORDS MATTER

My divorce left a hole in my heart and a hole in the hearts of my two daughters. To avoid such a wounding, one tries to find a way around divorce. But it all comes down to which carries the most pain and damage: staying with your partner or leaving. I was convinced that the marriage was over and that staying together would do more harm than good for all involved. Convinced of this belief, I found the courage to leave.

After three decades-plus of being married, it was quite a change to learn to live alone and do all the chores the other partner used to do. For me, I had to learn a little cooking. (I really didn't know much about it and still don't.) The house cleaning came easily because I grew up helping my mom. I caught on to laundry quickly, too, but never learned to sew on a button. I farmed out this chore.

After making the furniture salesperson's year and learning my way around Williams Sonoma, my downtown condo looked like a gentleman's apartment. Lots of wood and leather—a small consolation for the bitter fight ahead as the separation proceeded into legal wrangling.

The side that initiates divorce and moves out first seems to pay the biggest price with the kids, no matter their ages. They don't understand, and how could they? The unhappy marriage was kept to a simmer, rarely boiling over. But the bitterness comes out in lawyer-speak at divorce hearings. Bad things, many untrue things, are said. The lawyers do a good job of ignoring the emotions and getting down to the facts for the decree document. In our case, there was little to be said about custody of children since our two were grown women.

For the woman I would eventually date and marry, it was a bit more complicated since her daughters, Alex and

Linz, were still at home. When I met them, Alex was fourteen and Linz twelve.

My divorce shredded the emotions of my two daughters, and M's divorce did the same to Alex and Linz. Parents try to protect their children from such trauma, but in divorce the pain is inevitable.

I first met Alex downtown. M, Alex, Linz, and I had paid a visit to our local bookstore on Union Avenue. This was considered a fun outing since at least three of us would just as soon read as eat. Alex was an attractive and bright young lady and had the mannerisms of someone on stage. She glided through a room, talked a lot, and became the center of conversation when around her mother and sister. She entertained.

Alex also possessed a sharp wit, effectively landing jabs at her targets. This wit, combined with my lack of understanding of her, would bring us to our relationship's crossroads. I was not sensitive to all her changes and emotional turmoil. I was also so different from most of the other people in her life that finding common ground was difficult.

As my relationship with Alex's mother progressed from magical courtship to wedding, it turned out that I would not have the opportunity to get to know Alex very well. She was not around as much as Linz, and I would say we were still pretty much unknown to each other on the day of the wedding. I watched Alex deal with the trauma of divorce with wisdom beyond her young age. In spite of her deep pain, she worked hard at forgiveness and to her credit emerged one day ready to start fresh with her mom. I think this was also an opportunity for me to begin building a deeper relationship with Alex. I didn't take this opportunity as seriously as I should have. Somehow, I just thought in time we would all blend together as a family unit. This was naïve on my part. Blending divorced families takes a lot of attention and purpose.

Alex and I were polite but not warm toward each other. I would ask M what she thought was the problem. Her first response: "Well, you are so different from what the girls are used to. It's going to take some time and energy." And it was true. Her dad, whom she rightly loves deeply, is quite different from me. I am bookish and contemplative, an introvert of sorts and cave-ish more than I care to admit. Alex, even though she is a serious person, was used to laughter and lightness around the house. Words of love and hugs of affection were common in her childhood, neither of which came easily to me.

I grew up in a household where my dad didn't tell me he loved me until I was around fifty years old. It was understood but never said. With my daughters, this was different. We used love language but not excessively. That language was usually reserved for holiday cards or when they went back to college. Using the word *love* too frequently seemed like it would diminish its meaning.

There was only one person in my life where I had crossed the love language barrier, and that was M. From the beginning of our courtship, I decided I would tell M I loved her every time I felt it. I didn't know I would feel it many times a day! However, it would be a while before I would risk saying the love word to my stepdaughters.

I had set up a consulting company in my home as I left the corporate world. M says it may have saved my life. My CEO job working an eighty-hour week with high levels of stress had taken a toll. Working from a home office was awkward at first. Not having any staff challenged me to become more self-sufficient with business tools. I had to learn how to become functional with a computer. It was hard. Then one day Alex came to my rescue. I now had someone who could type reports, make computer files for documents, make PowerPoint slides, and do Excel spreadsheets. Alex saved my bacon.

She basically became my competent administrative assistant, performing her duties with her typical perfectionist standards. Of course, I was pleased. As we worked together, Alex would ask me questions about the business. She was curious, and I was glad to give her some insight into what I did for a living. We gained mutual respect and friendship over that six-month period. But friendship had not grown into deep family love.

A few months later we faced a crossroads. We had picked at each other one too many times, and our relationship was in trouble. M was saddened by our behavior. We both loved M deeply and wanted to find a way to get along, if not for our sakes, then for hers.

I slowly began to realize that I was responsible for much of the mistrust in my relationship with Alex. Had I really shown her or said to her I loved her, the relationship would be better than it was.

M got us to sit down together and be honest with each other and say how we truly felt we were being treated. The other person listened and then responded. This helped a lot because Alex and I were, for the first time, able to clear the air. Later that same evening M explained to me that Alex needs for "you to say it, to say you love her."

I replied, "I do love Alex, even if I don't say it much." M knows I have had a love language barrier, although not with her.

I thought this over and decided, I am going to say it to Alex every time I feel it, just like I do with M. It turns out I felt love for Alex often. As she heard these real and important words, she began to respond with loving words, too. We were making progress!

Several years have now passed. The bond is stronger between Alex and me. Together, we have built the "circle of love": moving from saying "I love you" to developing a closer bond, to feeling the love more, to saying it more. Just like actions, words matter.

JACKSON'S FAVORITE SISTER

M came to me when her younger daughter was in the ninth grade. She asked me to watch a slide show Linz had prepared titled, "Why we should get a dog." I think M had coached her daughter that her stepdad would need a strong persuasive argument if he were to ever agree.

My argument for a pet-free zone was quite rational: no animal hair, no poop in the house or yard, and no caretaking that would eventually roll downhill from daughter to stepdad. I had been through this all before with my own two daughters when they were in elementary school.

The bargain at that time was to borrow the cute little

fluffy kitten for a day. Right. On the second day, the cries were, "Can we keep him? We promise to take care of him." So JJ joined the household. But when JJ wouldn't let the girls hold him, they lost interest. He shed, I vacuumed. I fed him. I changed his litter box. I did this and more—for the next eleven and a half years.

Eventually JJ was pushed into the garage. At least I could contain the shedding. The winters were cold in Ohio, but JJ survived. Usually when you care for a creature, you grow a bit fond of it. And I did. In good weather, JJ would join me on the back deck and bask in the sun. We spent many evenings quietly looking at the woods and sometimes each other.

A couple of days before JJ's death, we had this cosmic experience: JJ stared straight into my eyes as if our souls were communicating. I sensed our time as friends was coming to an end. A couple of nights later, he got into a fight with another animal and was torn to shreds. I sadly buried his remains. Stricken with pet grief, I vowed never to have a pet again.

Now I was faced with another argument for pet

ownership. The slide show impressed me. Linz had worked hard on it. In fact, I have to say she worked harder on that slide show than any school project at the time. Linz made lots of good points for her case, from "man's best friend" to "guard dog." This latter argument scored points given the compulsive deadbolt locker that I am at night. She, of course, promised total responsibility for the pet, as all children do. She made this promise without realizing that in a few years, the dog would be left to us as she headed off to college. However, this fact of life did not escape my decision.

Family blending after divorce is no small task. Linz and I were trying, but the moment of "we're a family" hadn't occurred. For this reason, if for no other, I wanted to grant her request. But I kept thinking of all the animal hair, the poop, and all the caretaking I would end up doing, no matter Linz's good intentions.

I also understood I could bond with a dog. After all, I bonded with JJ. I also remembered that to love a pet would someday mean the loss of that pet. A broken heart is almost always in the future with pets.

Linz was unhappy, of course, when I gave her the negative answer. But to her credit she treated my decision with respect. I think M thought I might give a bit, but no, instead I declared the house and yard a pet-free zone. This soon became problematic when the other set of parents gave her a dog, to keep at their home. M feared Linz might give up some of her time with us to stay more at her dad's. Again, to Linz's credit, she did not do this. She continued to rotate to our house as planned and kept trying to find a way to connect with me.

Over the following years, Linz and I would have our ups and downs. It was not easy blending a not-so-neat teenager with an uptight, compulsively neat stepdad. M, the peacemaker, had her work cut out for her.

When Linz left for college, M grieved. I remember this grief when each of my daughters left for college. Each time it lasted about a year. Perhaps, I thought, a dog would be a good thing, something for her to hold onto and love as she grieved over the departure of her youngest. I went to M and offered to tolerate a dog if she wanted to get one.

On her next birthday, M purchased a puppy for herself. The pet-free zone became "beware of the puppy poop zone." The poop accidents would go on for months. And I never walked so much in my life. Fortunately, M adopted a shed-free breed—thank God for small favors. We named the pup Jackson. It was a noble name for a very small dog.

Linz came home from college for the summer and loved Jackson from the start, and he loved her back.

Somewhere during this time Linz and I came to an unfortunate juncture in our relationship. We still were not family-bonded. The incident involved me blowing up over her not being packed by bedtime the night before she was to return to school. She had invited a friend over, and there was more talking than packing. When I discovered she was not ready, I became irate. My anger was too hot, way too hot—way, way too hot.

It would take me months to see how much I had overreacted and for Linz to process her hurt. M would be the patient bridge between us. We would go to therapy together, and to Linz's credit she would forgive me. Our relationship was transformed.

At first, the fur ball M purchased fit into the palms of our hands. As an adult, he grew to a height of twelve inches and a weight of thirteen pounds. Jackson had a black face, white body, and a large black spot on his back and side. He gets all the compliments in the family. Literally everyone thinks he is very cute.

Luckily for Jackson, and for me, I worked at home, and we have spent about every day of his life together. His favorite game, "pitch the pig," involves the stuffed pink pig Linz gave him. I think it was one of her favorite toys as a child. Jackson and I also wrestle in the floor, as boys should do from time to time—usually over M's objections.

As it turns out, Linz had understated my future relationship with a dog when she said in her presentation, "Dogs are man's best friend." Jackson is more than my best friend; he is family. Linz and Jackson have a special relationship, too. When Linz visits, he recognizes her car as she drives up and the celebration begins: the jumping, the barking, an excited drip of pee, all for Linz.

It is clear: Linz is Jackson's favorite sister. We have recognized this legally in our will. If anything happens to us, Linz will become Jackson's guardian. He is a lucky dog.

Jackson just had his fourth birthday when I discovered my stage 4 cancer. I had been dreading the day of pet grief. Poor Jackson. It looks like he will have to be the one who feels the grief of loss. I don't think Jackson and I have had a cosmic relationship, but we have loved each other dearly.

And now the great comfort to me is that Jackson will have M and his favorite sister to help him fill the void, just as I would have had if the cards were dealt the other way around.

AM I MY SISTER'S KEEPER?

We were as close in age as two siblings can be without being twins—born ten months apart. Brenda showed our Scottish DNA with wavy auburn hair and freckles across her nose. I showed the German ancestry with pure blond hair and bright blue eyes. Not only did we not look like siblings, but our personalities were on the opposite ends of the emotional-rational spectrum. Brenda felt everything deeply and I, well, I lived in my mind and didn't feel enough. Our brother, Glenn, who came along a couple of years after Brenda, looked more like her and would live a life of zest and passion, daring to go to new frontiers.

Due to the youth and immaturity of our parents, I ended up being the third parent at age twelve. This role was not always appreciated by my siblings, since I could be direct and bossy. (It would have saved time if Brenda and Glenn had always just agreed that I was right.)

To play together with two brothers, Brenda would have to pretend to be a soldier or a cowboy; her brothers had little interest in playing her sissy games. When Brenda was eleven, she entered puberty and grew bigger and stronger than either Glenn or me. We learned to respect her a bit more or she would smack us.

I was a slow reader in elementary school, but Brenda was even slower. I remember the three of us sitting in the car outside our elementary school building while Mom was inside talking to the teacher. When mom returned to the car, we learned that Brenda was being held back a year. There was no way around it: we viewed her failure as a family stigma.

Despite making pretty good grades and graduating high school, Brenda, unfortunately, didn't feel smart in school. We, her family, failed to help her set higher expectations for herself. Many times, people live down to expectations. Still, Brenda would regain some of her self-worth later in life through her artistic side.

As Brenda grew into an attractive young lady, Dad would set strict boundaries for her. Since he himself was an untrustworthy man when it came to young women, he projected this onto every suitor. These boundaries for Brenda were much stricter than the boundaries set for me or our younger brother. Brenda wasn't allowed to "like" a boy until she was sixteen. She also developed a sharp tongue for Dad's commandments. This was not good, because Dad was given to sudden and explosive anger. I vividly recall the switching in the yard she received when she was sixteen for talking back.

Brenda would make some poor choices once she was out from underneath our father's heavy hand. In her early twenties, these choices would lead to her being told by Dad that she was no longer his daughter. I can't imagine the pain she must have felt when, year after year, her father made it clear that he was disgusted and didn't want to see her.

I don't really know why I didn't go to Dad on Brenda's behalf and try to reason with him. Maybe it was because we all knew he wasn't reasonable, and he would stubbornly hold to his unjust opinion of Brenda. Besides, he was sure to be angry, and I wanted to avoid the same wrath he dished out to his daughter.

Brenda would eventually come to say she hated Dad. Who could blame her?

Other men would mistreat Brenda, from the husband who abandoned her when she was pregnant with my nephew, to the man or men who raped her. Brenda's life was one of woe. From a combination of bad luck and bad choices she would spiral downward. There were moments of light when she would hold down a job, but the moments of darkness overshadowed these.

Brenda always held me in high esteem. I would visit and try to help her in her troubles but only to a point. I couldn't be distracted from climbing the education ladder and then the corporate ladder. Her high esteem was misplaced.

I have saved a voice message from her on my phone

from March 2013, a short time before she died of cancer. She was begging me to call her. I'm sure I briefly called her, but I didn't go to see her in her final days. I can't now remember the business meeting that kept me from driving four hours to see her.

Brenda's son, Tim, is a man she would be proud of, despite the trauma of his childhood. He is exceptionally bright, a graduate of Auburn, with a successful career. I remind Tim from time to time that I went to Lamaze classes with his mom and was there in the waiting room at his birth. I remember decoding a computer program while I was waiting for Brenda struggling in labor.

Dad, Tim's grandfather, stepped up to the task and helped raise him. In many ways, Dad has been to Tim the father he never was to his daughter. Dad thinks of Tim as a third son, and the relationship has enriched both their lives.

The cancer DNA runs in our family—from my maternal grandmother to my mother to Brenda and now to me. As I go through the treatment wave after wave, I am surrounded by people who care for me. My support network is broad and deep. This was not the situation for Brenda eight years ago. Many missed the opportunity to help Brenda and I am among them.

Tim, Brenda's son, is successfully climbing his own corporate ladder. However, he seems to be learning at the same time the value of staying connected.

THE LANGUAGE OF GOD

The question isn't do we believe in the Divine

but is the Divine manifest in our experience?

When I began my spiritual journey, I was sitting in a hard oak pew in a Baptist church. I was fourteen, having been baptized three years earlier, and a devoted youth for Christ. I recall a Sunday service where I distinctly remember feeling the Presence. As I sat in a church pew on the left side near the front during the sermon, a warm energy filled my heart and tears ran down my cheek. This feeling was new to me.

I went home mystified by the experience and told my mom about it. She had been in the service, too, but I had sat alone on my pew. Teenage boys didn't sit by their moms during a church service. My mom wasn't sure what to make of the experience but knew it must be good, so she asked the pastor to visit us. Pastor Lee showed up in our small sparsely furnished living room a day or two later. After I relayed my story, he knew exactly what had happened. With great confidence he announced, "You received the calling!" The calling to the highest of vocations: to be a minister, a pastor, a preacher of the Word.

As any fourteen-year-old boy devoted to his church and who implicitly trusted his pastor would do, I accepted without question this analysis of the situation. My mom celebrated. There was now a preacher in the family.

Reverend Lee took me under his wing and nurtured me in the ministry. He guided me to sign up for night Bible classes at the local Baptist association building. I was by far the youngest participant in this small class of a dozen people preparing to be ministers. We studied an overview of the Old and New Testament. In addition, I went to church six times per week if you count Sunday school and Training Union, which was like a second Sunday school before the evening service.

When I was sixteen, Pastor Lee began asking me to "fill the pulpit" whenever he was out of town. Apparently I did an adequate job, because he began recommending me to other local pastors as their fill-in. Eventually I would preach in most of the Baptist churches in Morgan County. Pastor Lee went a step further and worked with the deacons to have the church sponsor me as a licensed minister. I was a homegrown preacher boy. It would be years before I realized the lack of wisdom in this series of events.

This path led me to attend a Bible college, which may have furthered my knowledge of the Bible but did not prepare me to be spiritual. It also pushed me away from my culture so that, in time, I would be so out of touch I would have no idea how to really minister to the needs of others. The Presence would come and go over the years. The more I rationalized and intellectualized the Presence, the less I felt the manifestation of the Divine.

At twenty-three I had served several churches as

youth pastor and once as a Methodist circuit preacher. I was working full time in a grocery store and attending seminary part time. One day it dawned on me that the warm positive energy of the Presence seemed to be distant not only from me but also from most of my professors and fellow seminarians. Fortunately, I had enough insight to see that I must leave. I became a seminary dropout and never went back to the ministry for pay. I was a disappointment to my family, my in-laws, and my Baptist church.

Eventually I earned a teaching degree, taught history, and volunteered to teach and preach at my local church. This worked until our firstborn was due and I knew that, to support my family, I would have to leave teaching. It was the second career path I had tried and was now changing.

Through a set of circumstances that still seem providential—although I am certain such a thing doesn't exist and the word is usually poorly defined—I ended up in health care. After an MBA and a promotion to an executive job, this became my career and more than met the needs of my family. In whatever church we attended, I continued as a volunteer teacher and preacher. Eventually I helped plant a new church in Cincinnati but made my living as a hospital executive while continuing my self-education in the Bible, theology, and philosophy. It became a hobby for decades. I never lost a passion to know more about the big questions of life.

My knowledge of religion continued to increase but not the Presence. It seemed the more I learned in books, the more I became disconnected from my emotions and my heart. This lasted until I became an elder and teacher in the megachurch. At this church there was a renewed emphasis on knowing God experientially, not just knowing about God. In time I would reconnect with the warmth I felt as a teenager sitting on a hard oak pew. The tears that had dried up long before returned. My emotions were reconnecting to the rest of me.

This reconnection opened me up for the experiential knowledge of the Divine to become a daily Presence in my life. Meditation and the silence of contemplation opened my mind and heart to a daily walk with the Divine. This has not only increased my spirituality over the last twenty years but has also decreased my respect for religion, church, and doctrine.

I have come to know the ultimate truth of the Divine and the ground of reality. I have also become convinced that statements of faith are not spirituality; rather, spirituality is in the manifest experience of an encounter with the Divine. This kind of spirituality does not require a leap of faith. It is more real than that.

I have found the Divine in the unexpected place within my inner self. I have heard the Divine in the sounds of the ocean's vastness. I have seen the Divine in the timelessness of Sedona's red canyons. The Divine speaks in this awe and in the warmth of a teenage boy's heart. The language of God is not in the sermon on Baptist theology. The language of God is in the experience of warmth and awe. It is in the encounter with the Presence.

VISITATION FROM A BAPTIST MONK

Some say that my teaching is nonsense.

Others call it lofty but impractical.

But to those who have looked inside themselves,

this nonsense makes perfect sense.

And to those who put it into practice,

this loftiness has roots that go deep.

—*Tao Te Ching*,

translation by Stephen Mitchell

I was at Bobby Lockwood's gravesite on top of a hill above Tellico Dam when Bobby prayed for my cancer to be healed.

Bobby Lockwood was someone I knew in Bible college. My real connection to him was through his sister, Judy, the wife of Jerry DePoy, my college roommate and longest friend on a continuous basis. Jerry and Judy were with me on the hill as I stood near Bobby's grave.

Bobby was the big man on campus, a proper pastor, wearing a white shirt and tie, carrying his Bible under his arm wherever he went. He was personable and kind to everyone he met. He truly had the pastor's heart. Just about every student of the five thousand on campus knew of Bobby's monkish devotion to our triune God, and as a result, he easily was voted president of the student body.

Jerry DePoy admired Bobby and ended up marrying Bobby's sister, then following in Bobby's footsteps to also become a Baptist pastor with a big heart. Over those years, I have changed my views toward church, religion, and politics. Jerry has remained firmly grounded in the faith.

We have always been an odd couple even when we

were roommates, but we remained warm friends by talking only a bit about our different views on religion and politics. We are authentic with each other but careful to be respectful and not let the serious discussion go on too long. There were always more important things to talk about—like Jerry D's most recent church jokes or our days of flirting with freshman girls at the "Happy Corner," the college hangout.

The gravesite experience came about this way: I had called Jerry a few months prior and told him about my cancer. The big-hearted pastor insisted on making the ten-hour drive to see me while I had energy for the visit. He and Judy came to our home to stay a couple of days and share life with me and make some more memories.

The first night Jerry and Judy were having dinner with M and me, Judy said she would like to visit her brother's gravesite. Years before, Bobby had moved to our city and pastored a local Baptist church. He had died suddenly of a heart attack, and since his death, Judy and Bobby's wife, Linda, had drifted apart. Judy had not seen Linda or Bobby's gravesite for years. I thought the idea of visiting Bobby's gravesite was a splendid idea, although I had to nudge a reluctant Jerry D to fall in line and go with us the next day.

To find the gravesite, Judy contacted Bobby's widow. Linda had taken the death of her husband very hard. It had taken her a long time to come out of her depression and loneliness. Bobby had taken care of most duties during their marriage, leaving Linda unprepared to navigate life on her own. In her withdrawn state she had pulled away from Judy and others. Linda and her son, Lee, who happened to be home at the time, agreed to meet us and take us to the gravesite.

We met at the Starbucks in Lenoir City, close to Tellico Dam. I thought it would be a five-minute reunion and then we would follow them by car to the gravesite. However, it turned into an hour and a half memorial discussion. Normally this might bore or irritate me, but it didn't. Rather, we celebrated this person who had had great influence on the lives of his family. I was the outsider but joined the conversation whenever appropriate. By the end of our long, joyful conversation, I felt like an insider. Lee, the son, commented that I had a "gentle spirit." This meant a lot to me. To share and love and rejoice with these Lockwoods brought deep meaning to my day. I truly have been transformed through my painful journey with cancer.

We drove to the gravesite, and I was awed with the beautiful natural setting of the grassy hills and trees high above Tellico Lake near the giant structure of the dam. As we walked from our cars to the top of the hill where Bobby's remains had lain undisturbed for eighteen years, I stumbled. I caught myself from falling by reaching out and catching Lee's shoulder. It was like he, too, was an old friend instead of a new stranger.

Reaching the marker, I read the inscription: Rev. Bobby Lockwood, 1953 to 2003. I realized Bobby and I were born in the same year. Bobby had always seemed older and wiser than me, but he was just twenty years old back in Bible college when he was admired by the student body. As the four relatives shared more stories and joys of Bobby's life, I felt compelled to excuse myself. I walked up along the tree line to the top of the hill out of the sound of voices and meditated about Bobby.

After a few moments of silence, breathing in the environment, I could visualize Bobby's face. In another few moments, I began to feel an energy, his energy. And soon, I felt this spiritual image of Bobby praying with me to heal my cancer. His presence was as real as those back at his gravesite. I enjoyed the warmth of his presence and the energy he sent my way from his spiritual world.

When returning to the group, I said, "It turned out I didn't meditate about Bobby. I meditated with Bobby." I felt that way the rest of the day as I intermittently visualized his face. I had, in my view, a visitation from the Baptist Monk.

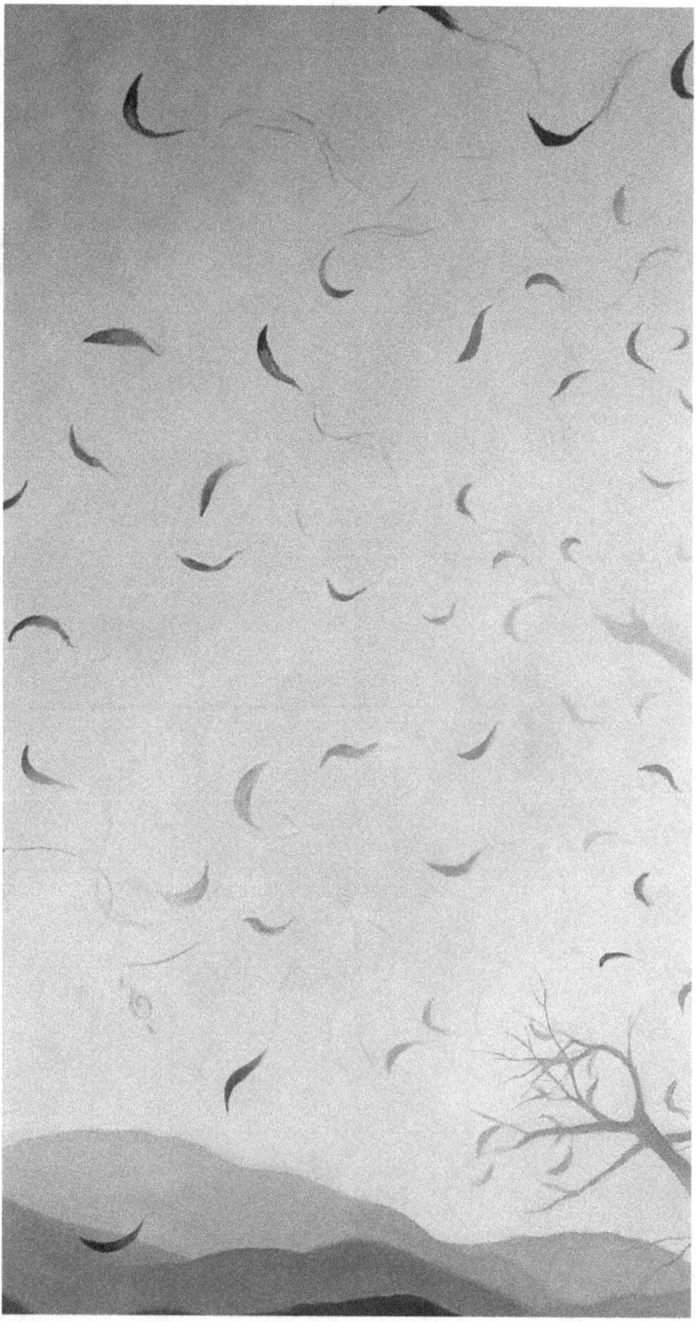

TELLING MOM

At seventeen, on a September morning, my mother had pushed me from the warmth and safety of her womb. The cutting of the umbilical cord may have divided us physically, but we would remain attached in so many other ways. She became my caregiver, first teacher, and eventually trusted friend.

I remember my mom taking us to her mom's apartment on Cicero in Chicago. My Grandma Tootsie was a large woman with a kind and loving manner. Grandma made us homemade apple turnovers while we played in her living room. The apartment was open, so she could see my sister and me from the kitchen as we played on the floor with cars, soldiers, and dolls. Later, when I was nine, Grandma Tootsie died from breast cancer. She suffered two long years with the dreaded disease. I remember singing carols to her on her last Christmas as she lay in her bed.

The stories are told and retold about her sainthood as a wife, mother, and grandmother. Perhaps overstated but maybe not. My grandfather Bud certainly thought Grandma Tootsie was a saint and for years looked forward to joining her in heaven. My dad now, as he ages, thinks of my mom as a saint, too. These men, not so good at being husbands, certainly believed their wives to be loving women.

Both my mom and Grandma Tootsie found their faith a sweet rescue as they lived with harsh men living out the patriarchy of their era. For this, I also count my mom among the female saints of our family. She gave a lot to her family and husband of almost seventy years and counting. Like a lot of southern women, she may have given too much for her own good.

In her early seventies, my mom also developed breast cancer just as her mom had in her late forties. I clearly remember staying in the hospital room with her the night after surgery. As anyone knows, the few nights and days after major surgery involve a lot of pain. I held her hand as I lay in a chair beside her bed.

The attachment to her never felt stronger than that night. Now, over fifteen years later, every time I hug her this strong feeling comes back, bringing tears to my eyes. Until that night in her hospital room, I think I had not fully appreciated the sacrifice she had made in raising me. We all say we appreciate our moms on Mother's Day, but do we really feel that appreciation deep within our souls? I think not, at least not until we face a crisis with our moms, and then I think it really sinks in.

One of my hardest days in life came a couple of years agon when, on my sixty-fifth birthday, I committed her to a nursing home. I was the only one who could convince her this was for the best. She went, but not without an emotional struggle. It was hard to give her over to the nursing home, but in hindsight, we all agreed it was for the best. Every time I visit her there, I must remind myself that the nursing home's care has extended her life and, yes, even provided more quality of life as she strolls the halls, speaking to everyone she meets. I think she would have died of loneliness if she had continued living with my dad. Besides, he can hardly take care of himself from his wheelchair, let alone take care of his wife with a failing memory.

In June 2021 I traveled to Alabama to visit my mom, the first time since COVID hit. I had to bring the news of another sad event in our lives: my cancer.

Having just arrived, M and I—wearing masks and sterile gowns—sat in the nursing home dining room along with my mom. My mom started the conversation. "Jerry, you are getting older. You need to make sure you are taking care of yourself."

M and I looked at each other, having the same thought. Mom had unknowingly given us the opening to tell her our bad news. When I said, "Mom, I have bad news," she looked straight into my eyes and responded, "I knew you didn't look well." Now I didn't look bad. I still had my hair, and I still weighed about the same. How mothers always know our secrets, I can't explain, but it seems a universal trait. We didn't tell her that the cancer had accelerated from stage 3 to stage 4, but we did tell her I had cancer and was in treatment. She told me (as if I didn't know), that she had survived cancer a decade ago.

We moved on and chatted about the usual stuff for the next thirty minutes. Then the nurse came back and said our time was up. As I departed, I held my mom tight and cried. I wondered if this would be the last time I would see this sweet person who means so much to me. She is part of me, and I am part of her. If I go first, I will be there with Tootsie to escort her to the gate, and if she goes first, I know she will be there for me.

The Sounds and Scratches of Death

"Accepting one's own death" is a bold assertion. How do you do this? Life is clearly a gift: none of us who have it made it happen, nor did we earn it.

One day as a small child I became aware of me—the me looking out from my soul to see through my body's eyes, to see the world. The context of my experiences was forming a framework of meaning in my mind. Helping me build that framework, my mom said, "Jerry, can you say *dog*?" and pointed to a dog. Eventually I could say "dog" and point to a similar animal that I had associated with the word. I was learning the meaning of these sound-symbols.

A teacher said, "See Spot run," and pointed to these letter symbols on a page of a running dog with spots. I was learning how to associate these scratches—these written strokes—with letters, then sounds and words, and finally their real objects. My mind was processing its experiences into meaning. I was meaning-making while learning the process of the correspondence of symbols to reality: *dog*, the symbol of the real dog.

This is how our minds use layer after layer of experience to make meaning of reality. It is easy to forget that the sound or letters for *dog* are not really a dog. It is easy to forget that the sound and the written scratches of *dog* and correspondence to a living dog are limited. The word approximates but doesn't wholly translate the essence of the thing itself.

The word *death* is of course just sounds and scratches of the real thing. And the word, of course, is limited in the meaning it conveys about the essence of death.

In *2010: The Year We Make Contact*—sequel to *2001: A Space Odyssey*—Hal's professor-creator holds a serious conversation with Hal, a nonhuman artificial intelligence character. He says Hal will have to give up existence for the purpose of the mission and the survival of the crew. Hal has only one quiet, moving question for his maker, "Will I dream?" The good professor levels with Hal and replies, "I don't know." Hal accepts death. The word *death* is just sounds and scratches. The android Hal is only bits and bytes, but his experience is real.

My oncologist, when asked how long I would live without treatment, said "four to six months." He, too, said this quietly and honestly. In *2010*, the professor honored Hal with dignity, and in life so did this doctor honor me. Unlike Hal, I didn't ask my doctor, "Will I dream?" The word *death* I heard in my doctor's statement was only sounds and scratches, but I am more than bits and bytes.

I don't have to ask my doctor if I would dream, although it would be interesting to have heard his answer. I think I know, at least for myself, the answer. I know because I have touched the consciousness behind the universe in my meditation. Yes, it is mostly subjective, but many others in their mystical experiences have touched the same.

Death is the stopping of body but maybe not the

soul and the spirit. To quote an ancient book of wisdom, Job bemoans the death of humans and admires the resurrection of trees: "But when people die, their strength is gone. They breathe their last…" (14:10). In the same chapter, Job continues to bemoan the mortality of humans when he compares humans to a tree that resurrects itself by growing a shoot from its root. As much as I would like to think so, Hal probably didn't continue to dream. But for me, a living being, not a machine, dreaming is in my future when my body returns to dust.

Yes, the incomplete meaning of the sound and scratching of the word *death*, like Job, doesn't leave much hope. The usual meaning doesn't include a mystical encounter with the oneness of the universe. Yet, even with my mystical knowledge, it isn't easy to accept the reality of death just around the next corner.

I choose to try to accept this word, this word of "ceasing the body" and what it represents in leaving M and our daughters. Dear M writes to me today: "I think the more we can accept the reality of death, our own and others, then we are freer to embrace the life we have, in whatever form it takes. Reaching that place of acceptance seems to be an emotional and spiritual process that leads to more peace, more joy, and more 'space' inside for the wonders that life presents around every corner. Love and friendship and learning and laughing and crying … those wonders that are part of being alive." True wisdom from my partner.

I think I have found a way to accept death—not the sounds and scratches but the real thing. Science and religion agree that we came from stardust. Reality demonstrates that we evolved to have both a body and consciousness. My leap is that I believe spirit, or consciousness, is also in the deep structure of the universe. Therefore, my particles contain both stardust and consciousness. My body returns to stardust but my spirit to its home among the stars.

ACKNOWLEDGMENTS

This book was a calling for twenty years, yet it didn't take on reality until I met my divinity school classmate in Dr. Seow's Hebrew Bible class in 2019. Both of us were much older than our classmates, as evidenced by our mutual gray hair. Sitting together in the front row, we quickly became friends and have grown that friendship during this and other projects. As providence sent Aaron to be the voice of Moses, so has providence sent me an excellent writer to assist with my calling. Without Richard Sowienski, I doubt I would have had the courage to write beyond my personal journals.

The vulnerability, intimacy, wisdom, and support of my life partner, Melanie (M), is almost inexplicable. The only word that comes to mind to describe our relationship is *magical.* M is an expert in language and an editor in her own right. She diligently edited and re-edited this work of love for our daughters.

I would be remiss if I didn't mention Dean Judge at Vanderbilt Divinity School. His class on *Writing Creatively About Religion* gave me the confidence to write. Thank you, Dean Judge, for being a warm critic as I grew as a writer. VDS students are lucky if they can get into any of your classes.

ABOUT THE AUTHOR

J. W. (Jerry) Burgess, as a young man, pursued studies in religion and history. After graduating from Memphis University, Jerry taught high school history, a job he loved. However, with the approaching birth of his first daughter, he made a career change to the health-care industry. After earning an MBA from the University of Cincinnati, he served in executive positions in various nonprofit hospitals. Additionally, he founded a business coalition of health-care companies as well as a health insurance company providing coverage to low-income individuals.

During the last fifty years, Jerry has pursued his passion for studying theology and philosophy—not as a career but as a calling. In 2019, he fulfilled a longtime dream of enrolling in a graduate degree program at Vanderbilt Divinity School in Nashville. After the discovery in 2020 that he had colon cancer, he concentrated his Vanderbilt studies in creative writing, ultimately producing this book of essays dedicated to his daughters. According to Jerry, the joy, pain, and growth in writing these essays has enhanced his humanity and spirituality.

Jerry and his wife, Melanie, live in Knoxville, Tennessee, with their mischievous dog, Jackson. They have four daughters and two grandchildren.

Feel free to get in touch with Jerry via email at TreeOfLifeAndWisdom@gmail.com.